Jon Glover was born in Sheffield in 1943. He grew up in Surrey/South London and moved to study in Leeds in 1962. Apart from a crucial year in America in 1966–67, and many summers with his wife and children, and her family, in Upstate New York, he has lived in Leeds and Bolton, Lancashire, ever since. He has written four books published by Carcanet and two pamphlets of poems published by Northern House. He has edited with Kathryn Jenner *The Complete Poems of Jon Silkin* (Northern House Carcanet 2015). He is Advisory Editor of *Stand* magazine, and coordinates the Northern House books for Carcanet. He is Professor Emeritus in English and Creative Writing at the University of Bolton, Honorary Fellow of the English Association, and Honorary Fellow of the School of English, University of Leeds. He holds an Honorary Doctorate from the University of Bolton.

T0159824

JON GLOVER

Birdsong on Mars

CARCANET

ACKNOWLEDGEMENTS

Some poems have appeared in *Poetry
and Audience*, *PN Review* and *Stand*.

First published in Great Britain in 2020 by
Carcanet
Alliance House, 30 Cross Street
Manchester M2 7AQ
www.carcanet.co.uk

A CIP catalogue record for this book is
available from the British Library.

ISBN 978 1 78410 975 2

Book design by Andrew Latimer
Printed in Great Britain by SRP Ltd, Exeter, Devon

The publisher acknowledges financial
assistance from Arts Council England.

For Elaine Glover 1944 – 2019

and Abigail, Jerry, Alice, Oliver and Jake
and Rhiannon, Katie and Lizzie
and Nancy and Jackson, and Elaine's family members in New
York State including Katrina, Brian, Lowell and Colleen,
Jared and Alyssa

And to all those who loved and cared for Elaine
especially during April to September 2019
with special thanks to
the Doctors, Nurses and Volunteers at the
Bolton Hospice
the Spring House Surgery
and to staff of Orchid Care and of Home Instead

Most of the poems in this book were written before my wife Elaine's sudden illness. They include poems written from 2011, after the publication of *Glass is Elastic*, to the present. I found it irrelevant to write, or to try to write, from the Spring of 2019 till the Spring of 2020. On 23 April 2020, with no plan or intention, I picked up a pen and 'Pandemic' appeared. All twenty-six poems in the final section of this book were written between 23 April and 18 May 2020, concluding with 'Cold Blanket'. There are a few more words about these poems and their relationship with Elaine's death on page 125.

Jon Glover
30 May 2020

CONTENTS

Garden	3
Crass	4
Traps	5
Safety	8
Inhale	9
Bed-Time	12
Wrapped Up	14
Curved-In Stained Glass Windows	16
Bicycles	17
Chalk	19
Wild Flowers	20
Fries	22
What Waveband?	24
Decaying	25
Out-Drift	27
Instant Distant	28
Matter	30
Migration	31
Pleasure	32
Prescription Drug	33
Up Or Down	34
Last	35
Sick	36
Underneath	37
Autumn 1962	38
Free Flight	39
Art Shop	40
Paint Colours	41
Culture And Anarchy	42
Bone Vibes	43
Airwaves	44
Taste	45
Formulation	46
In The Sun	47

Drive-Thru   48
Meadow   49
Marrow   50
Untitled Art   51
Milk   52
Truthful   53
Tectonics   54
Pod   55
Canals   56
At Random   57
Frisson   58
Digitise   59
Estimate   60
Decorations   61
Synthetic   62
Salamanders   63
Chess   64
Haunting   65
Beaver Pond   66
Gardening   67
Three D   68
Listen, No, Look   69
Language Games   70
Transitory   71
No Colour   72
Colour Slide   73
Nice   74
August 2013 In Jefferson, N.Y.   75
Sunlight   76
Clock On   77
Putty   78
Spinning Top   79
's a Connection   80
Print Out   81
Closure   82

Birdsong On Mars   83
Ordinary   84
Intentions   85
Slow Messages. Slow Nerves. Staffa Again. Stop   86
Darkness   87
Written Smell   88
Trod. Romanesque   89
Contract   90
Ant Trails   91
Gone Viral   92
Captivating   93
Fugal   94
Utter   95
Scabs   96
Solstice Tinted   97
The Sea's Not Far   98
Therapeutic   99
Florid   100
North Wall   101
Groel   102
Trance Or Trope   103
Cogs   105
Weighted   106
Writing's Off   107
Hot Pee   108
Bed Bound   109
Ambulance   110
Guard   111
Drivers   112

WALKING STICKS

Looking At Drawings From Teretzin   113
Sticks   114
Pictures and Poems from Terezin   115
Sprocket Holes   116

Lupins   117
Re-Sus   118

Front Room Zoo   120
Past   121
Kitchen Knives: Homework: Signatures   122
Going Out. Right Out   123
Into the Archives   124

TWENTY-SIX MOCK SONNETS FOR ELAINE

Pandemic   126
My Mum's 1920s Hospital, Research   127
Cancer or Virus   128
Flying   129
Maths   130
Electric Sleep   131
Beloved   132
Diary Entries   133
Remains   135
Years Ago Appleton NY   136
Mock   137
Times Tables   138
Log Tables   139
So Long   140
Physics   141
Signs   142
Delaying   143
Tight Lipped Primary   144
Scans   145
Cold Blanket   146
Calgary or Appleton   147
Infirmary   148
Gave Birth   149
Fittings   150
Audubon   151
Back to the Beginning   152

GARDEN

I was pushed around Monet's
garden in a wheelchair. Mushy
views. Like the Science Museum's truths

they're not there. Impressions' faultless
loam. Pond-smells of distant creation,
it's rotting down, that's what it

does as the wheels go round, bumping in
history. The Japanese
bridges nearly tipped me out. There's

drifting through a looking glass,
earth's rotation on display as
gravity's squeak colourfully hurt.

CRASS

It was surely destined crass or sweet
to be running through memories
of art exhibitions. Brain

processes need filing as they
do with post-traumatic-stress
disorders. In the cabinet with

no way out. Bang shut. Papers
and oils and skins – printing, or sketching,
vellum with tattoos adoring

pastoral care. How could the recalled
impressionists, with Monet for
example, join in close like

a car crash? Always sorted. Fugues,
counterpoints pushing in with
sloppy colours. Vomit. What's to mop

up, to sip in cafés of
angry noise? Erotics. Just the art
of it in A & E headlong.

Or mis-filed bank statements. I use up
alternatives locked in for night
and day to add and subtract .

TRAPS

Why should Marseilles be
so strange as a set-
piece opening for
that novel? *Little
Dorrit*'s weather, names
and places all seem
diverted in the
first paragraph. I'm
lost already. Did
he get there? How did
he get there? Look it
up.
        So don't expect
London, railways, fog
or some industrial
waste. Hoping for cash
at the start, estates
or some other power-
space of an England
satisfactorily
gone astray or left
behind in a trap.
Tell time-travelling?
Those means of movement
studiously loved,
evoked, clip, clop, or
steam, demolition,

mapping out hot wet
gowns and stuffing, that
smelly leather shined
up from the slaughter-
house. Stench of headlong
destination – get
there in a week and
it's reduced to juicy
meat, boiling up
for circulation
in any head or
blood-flow or nervous
whiplash in the dark.

There now. Think of the
luxury or pain
of staring – over
and over: 'stared' three
times, 'staring' seven –
in those first few lines.
What an impression,
what an announcement
(Eighteen Fifty Seven)
of what might now be
judged Po-Mo playful
creativity:
just look at, and look
back, and be looked at.
Staring. The sun'll
get you. It knows what
it's looking for.

                    Though
I'm also stuck (can't
think it through) with young
Dickens' Buffalo
to Niagara
train trip, not knowing
what he would hear or
see till the carriage
door opened and there
was the roar of some
place invisible.
What's waiting's in charge
I think. 'No idea.'

SAFETY

Writing again in
a safe place or for
a safe place. Making
it to order as
Hughes did the lily
pad precisely lit
and green above the
mess. Nice and green though
unreliable.
Who would dare? Morals
of visualised
history. Drinking
the metaphors,
ecstatic bio-
ethics living it.
Old battlefields topped
with green, old skulls cracked
below well down and
invisible. Scots
bludgeoned into clean
fat metaphors or
bright Towton on the
desk. Study the fruit,
the flies, the meat blown
in the wind. Language
just goes on faster
than light through mountains,
quickest neutrinos
loving safety's home.
So no excuses,
it'll find you out.

INHALE

Breathing was waiting
to be a picture.

Stuff it. Where? Nailed up.
Picturesque. Picaresque.

Pictorial, all
these the same, bloody,

your oxygen held
up in a gallery

by screws and hooks or
cloaked high on a dead

person waiting to
be put away. Some

frigid cathedral
relics displayed hung

up and untouchable
so you can't feel the

cold, see the pallor
or wonder about

the atoms falling
off. Inhaling (halt)

exhaling, something
as a stop-gap, dropped

in the remaining
time slots, the working

hours in a day or
two, clock in, clock out.

Flat. Memorialising
the hot air. Placed as

a book is on a shelf
between kind others,

and removed and replaced,
removed and replaced

and read. Partially,
just one more new page

before the electrons
take another turn.

Tasty, swallowing
letters from the past,

to digest ex-voices,
library time supped up.

Some conversation
or democracy

working away on gut
strings beside vocal

cords for a song's low
ventilation, to air

out old backlog pacing,
to express and throw

away. I can't want
that pitch any more.

The real digresses.
Too slack, truth to say.

BED-TIME

Where's that music gone
now? Bed-time, up or

down for ever true. Hear
it still? Never, that's

not the point. It got
there in its own way,

flashy love brushing
air through the organ.

Measures stop air. Mud,
frogspawn, bubbles, trout

in the hushed dark in
your finger tips. O

K, mine. Hear the pulse
like soft, very far

thunder as the air
goes through. Breathe in, breathe

out and stop as though
it could finish in

silence and still be
there. Go on. Puff it

out and try to catch
the blank invisible

cushion behind the moon,
a journey that far

off, that soft, that cold,
a leather woodwind

instrument keypad
too fatty, too pressed

attentive to stir
colourless fluids

the acids in space,
but waiting. Dumb. Deaf.

WRAPPED UP

Triumphant, greener-
y, prize-like, wrap it

around my fingers'
cool fret to make a

rasping buzz. Hero-
ic. With a leaf, lips,

naturally, a
blade of grass stretched be-

tween my thumbs. Blurt it
out for all to hear

but me. Listening?
Hear it good. Hear it

from the inside of
muse or music, what's

played, written clearly.
Get in NOW. It's sur-

-rounding eyes' backplate,
retina wrapped up.

Cuddle it. Or drop
honey on your tymp-

anum. Listen in,
as they said, to radio.

Sweet ear, rolled fugues drum
in audible gold.

Sweet casting disson-
ance – stick your fingers

in each. Yeah. It hurts.
Warm and intimate

to end thus happy.
No? Stroke soft. Tierce

de Picardie. War-
fare brain barriers'

marginal defiance,
nerves' final endings.

CURVED-IN STAINED GLASS WINDOWS

Leaded lights with flowers
so middle class real
prim. Nineteen fifties

polished, if cracked through
trying to push the
bomb blast damage back

outwards. Suburban
explosions. History
framed as craft, as glass

picturesque. Handi-
work to occupy
strike time, like fine lace

or embroidery.
Or model balsa
aircraft hanging up

against the morning
light though they only
flew in your head. Grass,

geraniums and
lupins lean soft on
the gateposts. Freehold

years of democrat-
ised crap. Forbidden
wars. Not known, not owned.

BICYCLES

The man who fixed bicycles
wore a white lab coat. The man

who spoke loud from bottom stage
left to top seat right at re-

built Epidaurus was cas-
ually dressed. But muscles,

spanner tightening voice. Gears, change,
uniform, shirt-sleeves shout load

as if to go down the hill.
Can you hear? Larynx push out

happy screams. Or whatever
seemed to count. Down hill. Down time.

Puncture outfits sold well like
the end of a tragedy.

Jokes rise through the waves. Flounder-
ing saddle-sore pilgrims' irony.

Get there if you can before
it all goes flat. Again. French

chalk-out the sword play. I loved
the cycles hanging in the

windows. Or Chinese roast chicks
necks askew. Or tracts, buy one

for Paradise today if,
always if. Beaks at prayer.

Memories disjointed and
free-wheeling on purpose South.

CHALK

Pictures fill the time.
You do it, I do
it. Save the paper

and string. Bag it in
illustration so
accountably

prehistoric; the
garden worms, the moths
and micro-moths are

modelling sunny
survival. Smiling
godless on chalk towns'

slopes, artistic rots
they just about live
out. Southerly flints

glistening as heaps of
money do in a
drought-sucked cathedral.

Not fought through in care-
less chalk underground;
drained flight all past glass,

under glass. Museum
home-bound to value
comic-book style cash.

WILD FLOWERS

Brought to book and shelved,
left home well behind.
Seeded through my brain.

Privation scores high.
Plenty: count losses -
five, four, three, the rest

enjoyable and
gone over some edge
or other. Lost the

edge. Where is it? I
sniff for that depth all
rolled up. It's one glass

marble to score a
mystical drop? I'll
scream 'I've won': all right,

though bereft of sound.
Brightly halting ear-
drums, cataract-love

in focus far out.
Demanding, if I
could, all natural

worlds' parallel eye
tests. There, frigid bugged
results rise. Love the

planned egress trip way,
wired out, tip toes in
the dark, to excrete

into, or in, or
for oblivion.
It's quiet, so quiet.

A patterned ballet's
silent petals drool
damp skinside / airside.

FRIES

So unlike home. There's
an assertion, right.
Manhattan dockside.

No questions. All fright.
No worrying for
a past back gate or

garden fraud or the
last night's lit up Baked
Alaska prickling

for celebration.
What's left I think is
out alone at sea.

Goodbye ship. Goodbye
wet horizons. Lost,
un-lost. Memories

chew over i-dents
stamped, visa'd smells un-
familiar and

dreaded. Heat and weight
unloaded and re-
stacked for a car voyage

upstate so far out
and undiscovered
via Palisades, the

Jersey shore, and root-
beer. Drinks. Sugar-coat
donuts. Hot driving

North, driving West in
'Fallen Rocks Beware'
Zones. Nuclear Shelters.

Or 'Falling'. Obey.
Only natural.
It's the law like a

present in your hands.
Crackling to sweet taste.
Oblivion fries.

WHAT WAVEBAND?

Starting with Atlantic
voyages as subjects,

as fuel, as hot air.
Why need a log-on home

base for slave trades, the sweet
components of hoped-for

dementia, the out-of-
reach, the untidy and

gloomy? Been westwards and,
of course, north to realise

the Great Circle. Preening
imagination, then

let me out and down the
gangplank. Jurisdiction,

spinning the compass point.
All mine, all yours. Therefore.

DECAYING

It's my tempting and all-
authentic evocation:

replace landing places'
glossed memories in a

lovely world, to track where
the plane came down so hot

and carefully. Hush, hush,
comic strips of the fine

other life. Got 'em. Got
the exaggerated

pics because I subscribe.
I'm paying for extra

instalments way off in
the future. The story

'll be there, intricate
and zapping slick round the

planets. Oh freedom. Gone
through the retina catch,

iris recognition,
finger-print over voice

tone. Recording orbits
were there above the waves,

glowing like radium,
luminous watch hands tick

through and round desire. Time's
up. Wanting still lost speeds

planetary. Out there
for good, drift outnumbered,

thump dark, unpictorial
in every sunlight.

OUT-DRIFT

Breaking waves. When did they
start to do that? I mean
the words – crash, split, columns.

You choose, who chose? I think
of sunshine breaking through.
And a match, cotton thread

or plank of wood. The cells
of carbon, protein floss,
fibre just such as part.

Roses, fragmentary.
Yuk. Too good or clammy –
they block the phone lines or

flood past telegraph wires
petal deep. Some voyage.
Some interruption. Sun

light oceanic. Blood's
clear, transparency push.
Love's messaging out-drift.

INSTANT DISTANT

So there's another distant
island. Over the sea
unbothered. It's grey behind

the curve. Under the sky, clouds
frame it. Tap it to compose,
as the mobile phone says

on the screen within the screen.
Round the world is good enough.
I chose this landscape for its,

for its historic depriv-
ation. Justice or death for
me on the page. Too easy

pickings? Why that, why there? Why
some thorough, crude flattery
accrued? Convince yourself with

fancy talk that a hundred
years ago some dull starving
sufferers cared for you as

they might have found brief shelter
behind a wall with one last
candle before night won.

Why did I care for those lost
carers as though they loved my
bright future hash well worked for?

Fraudster with a verbal bank.
A landscape darling bereft.
I went for it like sunlight.

Sun-tan flatline messages
schooling a metaphor's blast
whilst sickening for something.

MATTER

The swallows fly past my ear
about three feet away. What
a noise. They're hungry. Am I?

What a feast! The quiets whir
like love so particular.
And again, sparring with the

air bits, sprinkling an inch of
sound, as one might imagine,
no metaphor, collisions

sub-atomic, so Latin
and proud with layers below
such grammatical benchmarks

we might know and use, use up,
and with midges splatter blood,
their bites used up for matter.

MIGRATION

Our winter, their summer. Timed
out. Shipping lines' disowned routes;
that is, no one owns mileage,

do they? Heroic plotlines
lace submarine pictorial
ties with compasses, trig points,

might they? Real estate mapped
as earthlike lines of force. Cheap
weight. Magnetic parameters.

However much star-gazing
I do, electricals won't
push to joined up. Metallic

beats, somewhere heartbroken sharks
heading South America –
wards. All hate and anger, fright

outlives migration. Back and
there. Got to get deep in the
map of particles. Driven.

It doesn't take very much
délicatesse. Calculate,
smell the legacies of breath.

PLEASURE

All that stuff light years away. Grazing
fish scales shimmering outward, try-
ing joy or silence. Thick-head,

you can't look it up. Look it out
outside. It ain't there, I'm sure,
though that's catastrophic certainty

and the stars won't like it, will
they. Giving them options, I see. Chew
things over. Cold, fatty fireworks.

Knock each other out with vibrating
waves or fields or equations right
turning blue for ever. Lose.

PRESCRIPTION DRUG

What would make you want to walk
somewhere, anywhere? Got to,
priceless diastolic and

systolic. And again. As
horse riders say, 'Walk on'. They
know it's good. All the balance,

wey hey, gravity loves the
rough stuff. A GP's sidelong,
(do I want 'sideways'?) glance.

Unspeakable prescriptions.
All accompanying form-
ulae and natural drug times.

Get it down you. What command!
And down till you lose count. Here
it comes again. Add it up.

Don't like the easy answers?
Numerical constriction.
And again, unquestioned yet.

UP OR DOWN

Home towards a rainbow might
allow desperate diversion.
So drive on straight through the light diffused.

Red's on the outside curve, recall.
Live the gears of rain. Ions so thrilling
and naturally speeding

up or down as you will or you don't.
Massed air governors go spin
through drops' pressed, colourful relief.

Think of dead weighing out the
distance to blue and indigo
creatures years away or outside time.

LAST

Autumn, last sunflowers.
Trash regrets, it's lost well out.
Stop regrets, it was all a construct

to make it worthless
or worthwhile whatever the
drugs or sunshine vitamins prescribed

for training to thought
free emotional black out
or some lucky midday auroras

so visible as
cookie cutter sonnets formed
through gratitude till it disgorges.

SICK

The sick came up quite perfect
grey bird's nest unfolding out –
wards. See it. It's surfacing, shine
to shine, as breath leaves its purpose
only heatless, heartless.

Did it know? Did it please? Acid
home comfort. Down there, it loves
itself and its particular
muscles and joy free progression
composition's drill.

UNDERNEATH

Underneath the library, corralled,
knowledge still and dry like mice singing
down this protracted circle
imaginative.

Open it up, with tin openers
or sardine-can keys, pattern you think,
so you refer for ever,
it's loveless, fallen

underground and cursed.
A pre-amble, a frozen
meal dramatically compressed, peat
bog falling, again rock-wise, mud-wise.

It will be frightened,
it will slush around like old
Sale Goods, redundancies low down there,
forgotten records, bar codes, tickets.

AUTUMN 1962

Did we ever unpick the 'Grammar' of
the Cuban Missile Crisis at the time?
Ownership, apposition – what a war
of hate and replicated fantasy.

Submarine linguistics. Try it on so
feared and fearless. We'd no threat to live it
and die it out. Superiors' games. A
cold autumnal revisiting of near

time wars, invasions real, and televised
to bring life's puppetry to life on hazed
and twinkling screens. As for those elected
to take the strain their atoms stink, archived

to be studied and reborn lovingly
with rhetoric's clamps and forceps smiling.

FREE FLIGHT

What has gone again? From bird song
left dry and homeless. Another day.
Unfed rhetorical blast

comes quickly though with energy
so consuming and unconsidered
it takes my breath away. Blood-

sucking air left just cornered.
All the sums corrected and no one
knows inside or outside the box –

ticks stay just too good to last
out the cold, and words for flight, and the
universe preening itself free.

Include yourself in time or myself?
Pick the true digits for their smell,
stinks right for birds or whale breath.

ART SHOP

Oil paint's leaden tubes touch. Squeeze
outline capital,
out-buy history's coloured tropes.

Some shop stocks new light's reflections,
banked clear for glory.
Perpetual choices flout

innards where floating
eye-marks take over in the
gray. Affordable prompts die out.

PAINT COLOURS

Roll up the lead tubes of carmine shine.
Availability of blood
dazzle's in danger, so

fold hot energy gobs
to savour. There's the liquid cost.
It'll dry and blank over. What's sure

and still flexible far inside
is some painterly gooey optic
nerve transporting slower.

CULTURE AND ANARCHY

Going out the door. Sloppy or
what! Possession
missing. Grammar allows
for some. Cultured word-shapes cool

odd anarchies. Perhaps. Get lost.
Inclusively
for all, not knowing where
multiplication tables

get truly beautiful. Lock 'em
and see. Never
in a million years out-
numbered, though tangible scum.

BONE VIBES

Gratitude for the trouble. Exceptional
sounds piss freely. Hear it again? Melancholy
goes without saying. Or any quick diagnostics.

You know its fixed in some bone vibes or other times
like the clock or tables or historicity tunes
I loved to learn. I know where you're coming from,

dead centre in the crystal set static crackling speech
or musical phrases from the ether - if
they knock you out that's fine. You'll know where you sure heard

not random or cadencing or flatline signs
of living priceless with fortitude for the print
or imprint or signage of worry while the moon's out.

AIRWAVES

Broadcasting, you're on, thoughtless transmission
by any old airwaves' scan.
Horizons outlived,

to overseas relentless,
pawned between the spaces
out there. Quantum leapt through excrement

of baggy planets
and their crude, flat, calculating jokes.
All aerials heave up their

pulses for good, for universal
thrift to make blood circulate,
just to knock it off.

TASTE

Procedural films
pass the time in cultural
capital. Behind barcodes loving

criminal circuits
for cash round the moon all night.
They could be space or nothing. Outright

entertainment sucks.
Think of the universe back-
firing loud to get a better taste.

FORMULATION

Floral universe,
good enough, I'd say, to lick
unless it's all gone wrong by itself:

robotic mistakes of fright
and beautification, like roses'
sugary clicking

on chocolates, astronomical
taste-buds planning the
end of the world together,

all breathless crying
with internal marigolds
ensuring the physics turns out right.

Crystallised violets
speak for attempted versions
of mathematical playfulness.

You've had your time out.
Wrap it, unpack it. With string,
or shining ribbon, something wants it.

IN THE SUN

There's some part of a marble
pathway, or granite, leading to
a fright of old bodies all decayed;

what a pilgrimage to the
underground, what vermillion
signs and redcurrant truths if the sun

could shine there as afterthoughts
sprinkled in the vault. (Don't know yer.
Unseen, thankfully.) Join the dots with

footsteps and footprints, and the fitting
sizes for width and length displayed
as logic truth tables flash.

DRIVE-THRU

Walking gets you healthy, it's promised,
or advised, for your choice, like heart-beats' drum stalks
talking aloud in your ears'

nonsensical construction. I wish
the ears', my ears', bones could step it out big time;
music of geometry,

seizing waves for their count down
or seizures in the decayed bits' transience.
Languages' footfalls. I like the fat,

the rubbish floating by quite
lonesome, despite its friendliness, its roadside
eats will get you without drive-thru tricks.

MEADOW

Think if a regatta from
the edge of the lake, the sound, the straits'
pretty wind for the eyes' print,
for the competitive beliefs in

the worth of silage versus next year's
seeds, and it's gone quite splendid,
as if you knew the rules of the game,
as if they had colour to

the end of the universe
and waves to leave flags drooping and beat
into the colour-coding
of a prize-winning meadow wanted.

MARROW

Leave it, for the tide's
gone. I like extra spacing,
good enough to add to the terror.

It's hardly worth the
fright, though. It's happening with
some pulse rates of half-speech and marrow.

UNTITLED ART

Signals from the gallery
walls come richly through
birdsong or what they do to protect

themselves. Speaking from the canvas in
some complex time frame
akin to possession buds

forming honestly antiqued.

MILK

The Hudson river was flat.
That's so romantic. Always meaning
too much by daylight

and, in whatever thought-free
geography you'd go for up front;
it's gone by with its

pearls and protestations, by
history and values sliding to the
narrows and the sea.

Or Narrows. Trade in flowing
water beautifies dissolved bear crap
and skin dust to milk.

TRUTHFUL

Trees have grown in pairs, relatively.
Though they might be miles
apart on far sides of the

Universe. Coo Coo. Come in, the time
shifts. Your time is up.
I love the forest's own plain

geometry. The stem-cells cultured
in the green and old
capillary attraction.

Just fancy it a bit. Why not? Blame-
free assuredly,
since grass and leaves flare truthful.

TECTONICS

Twenty eight miles till you dip
below horizons
from a seaside viewpoint at least. Old

hills flattened and grown again
volcanically
and magma burps into curvatures.

I love its joins and plasters.
Come on. You don't. Pre-
pretence to play with. Verbosity

enjoys tectonics. Fill out
with potential words
where you might go underground or sea.

POD

That will explode to milkweed
flowers and butterfly food honey –
sparks of white and frills.

Junk décor. Disney or what.
Nature's toys and amoretti's just
to be tasted. Bang

out silently drought filled needs
'urgency'. One of the words when you
have to pee out loud.

CANALS

Floods were like butterflies all
falling into place. When they need to,
when they can't do anything yet, so precise

and near to be ordered and
levelled. Water's fragility weighs
heavy. Sundown and breathless. The end of the

day comes from its chrysalis,
it's filling its wings colourfully.
It wants sleep now in canals to brightness.

AT RANDOM

I'm caught out dreadfully. Rude
talking insects wake
up. They're all

sexed up in my head too loud.
I fear the early
sonnets' shape

propping universal plans
with buzzed out structures
and planets'

revolutions round centres
chosen at random
and lost

FRISSON

Butterflies fidget.
Dignity
all heats up for the fall drop.

Would you like that to
look towards?
Fretting for the hot spot now

and then. Meaningful
tomorrow,
it's got to schlurp into the

art world's drinks' frisson.
Flattering
so the dread stops dead and squeezed.

DIGITISE

It's toylike, this tree with scabs of mosses and
liverworts and stuff that drinks what it can from airwaves and pipe
work. It's adopted for a toybox

in your ear canals, and talking aloud for
a stroke or a sip of juice or the clockwork to be wound up
as it does what it says on the seed

pack. Its metaphors play in the earth and matched
roots. Even if the jokes are nearly too self-consciously bad
for real, systemic irony. Come

off it! Digitise it – I wonder if
you could any more than it is already in its flagging
amiability and zeros.

ESTIMATE

Is any of it more beautiful
than its linguistic repeats
in my brain, or yours?

The most persuasive rhetoric digs
grave plots. It'll cost a lot
for a good view. Up

or down to the good
flat-line of nature's behest.
Who would estimate decay? Indeed?

DECORATIONS

Frightful green trees on offer on stilts on
waves of hardware for gardening acute bands

and angles of coloured tunnels outwards.
Where? Sumptuous air brushes shine aloud.

Get through if you want to like combing your
hair in a mirror naturally

dim and misty. Stuff all forests' wet and
multiple resources. I'm not

bothering with that. Branches of knowledge
scab and crust. For the new time,

new skin, new web. OK, you'll connect all
right in the leaf storm or

rain storm. I guess, don't try to map real trees,
or call them lovely or fond decorations.

SYNTHETIC

Old storms back up round here. Good
hills', good valleys' glacial
shapes are tender. No, I don't
believe that synthetic stitch.
Ain't no healing to caress.
The lingo don't. No tickle
or love making here abouts.
There's no power for this or that.
Alternatives frighten all.

SALAMANDERS

Off to see the beaver dam last night.
They might show up and splash their tails as
warnings to the family. Aliens
around. And they did, so I heard. I
didn't go. Too far round the squashy
pond and my shoes and legs wouldn't do
so much. But there they were plugging fast the
dam to make the trees more edible.
Teeth to ware down. So much, so little
of the world's scar tissue. Hold it in
while you can and then. Pipe work blocks. Try
fluent redeeming stents imagined
for an onward flow. Never mind though.
I saw salamanders on the floor.

CHESS

Some old mosquito bite was weeping.
Don't scratch, don't rub. Yellow stuff
on my towel from over my left ear.
Demands. Signals and skin-hollows.
Nuzzling chemical(s?) stand clear in their
networks. I wish they'd try another
to forge some flowery goo. It likes
dream of Scotland or Upstate NY
forests. Injury-free, in a sense,
but waiting the drains, the washing machine
make-belief of boundaries and stains.
Crease resistant, ironing free. I love
the coloured hole next morning,
still where it shouldn't be, proteins' chess.

HAUNTING

Haunting just doesn't do it. Repetitions
come flowering along. Daisy chains break out
in order. And come on back looking close
over a shoulder. Instant dissection,
immediately splitting the flower stalk
with a short nail. Here a face opens
with its natural edges? Placed, spit true
in place like a land I owe to the moon.
Unbelievable. Distorted hardly
from what wasn't there anyway. So wait
the finger-nail's next pressing. Juicy and
cutting alive for the doorway to some
room superior, do they say 'meta'?

BEAVER POND

To the beaver pond she walked this morning.
I heard it was flooding some more. Worthwhile.
It would be good to go there in the dark
and see the gaps, the pools and jaw imprints
as though some fire or abrasion or gun
shots were stroking clean rocks. Leave it for now,
though such chemical equations are so
tempting. Stick words in there and squeeze them tight
with molten nebulae and meaningful
systemic pressures. Got weak gravity's
poor old force plied in the dictionary.
Overnight, the pond's spread across the road.
Will power, the jawbones of the Milky Way.
I'm loving it, reeling it in on line.

GARDENING

Benign neglect has
turned into malignant neglect. Long
garden weeds fudge it.
Sugary compost gunk was winning
and over-layering
an old pattern from p'raps twenty five
years. We said 'oh no'.
It didn't need much space then, just wires.
It looks good from in
the library, from high up shelving.
Crafty earth sniffs clues.

THREE D

It's hard to know this silence.
The forest goes on and the wind is

delicate and easy, so.
Clouds up there move in their time and thick

space. Think of noise as a close
object's history, as a clay or tin

mug un-datable,
as leverage in scissors,
as cut-out, three-D paper-trails' weight.

LISTEN, NO, LOOK

Before you know it the colour's gone.
Or changed to some random opposite.
It's flooding again. And quite the all-
changed history to turn out this way. I'm
sure it's really hotter and the ice
is declining. It seems the leaves are
back to front and grass implodes into
pulp. Where is any colour chart or
order? Would I want it? If ever
light hand-cuffed between bricks or planks or
nail-heads could spark – or repent some new
time illumination. What's in there?
Untold regret of course. You climb in
there right now. Listen, no, look, it'll
solve your problems, don't think. About slide.

LANGUAGE GAMES

I don't like finding junk.
Or even to look for it. Why? Oh why?
All this, no, that, that gets sifted
and tossed stinks of the old.
The old days, the old colours, the old textures.
Smell the feel of fine clothes – all
the storage and washing and friendly
moth-balls. Time's dry skin casts,
the un-sexy shoulder flakes
the breath stitched in seams
with the richest of microbes.
In cupboards and drawers which
I see lined with yellowing news-
papers. Politics and theatre-reviews
under each heap of clothing – games,
or language games or folded
preparations. For how to use it all
again as any object will, or might
be then. Fitted with measuring tape
for the colours of blisters. The
weeping clear finish, the distance out.

TRANSITORY

White or paper or snow or shade or
mist or the inside colour of veins
or anything left behind un-shaded
in an old vacuum-cleaner bag –
it won't do, it won't do at all to
remember where the visual started out.
Like what won't be known or seen through enough
but from any shade of gray to a
fog on the beaver pond but nowhere else
seems today a step of disrespectful
trickery or a black cop-out or
unsaid desire from the cells backside
of sight. As though good calculations would
do all to erase the transitory.

NO COLOUR

The silence in this place when I'm
not there. Or the chair, the paper,
the final ink. I'm in the forest
as though in a first year tutor-
group, for easy, dead-end, repeat
philosophy questions handed out
or handed down. But Wittgenstein's
'Remarks on Colour', in my lap,
leaves me slow, stuck, as ever; white or
whitish, or pale gray, or fine gloss
sheets or leaves claim for anything.
Held tight, or divided for ever
between the shine and what's behind the
transparency that won't go home.

COLOUR SLIDE

Elaine said 'The white goes into the green.
It makes it disappear'. What did she
and Nancy see? What was lost and
what was left? There on the computer screen
it slid brightly. 'On', as fairy lights
or fireworks touching a finger end.
Blameless landscape acquisition. 'S'mine.
Tho' no one's hurt. Green, even if no-one's
too innocent, too languid or too poor.

NICE

Impatience is nice. I mean
free but rigid. It has to be
precise about the wanted, yet
not know how or when. Finely
loved, without any similes.
It's imprinted. It's words.
They're thoughtless. So want
the lot of it. Tomorrow should
come quickly. Should. Find
its necessity flying blind.

Yesterday, I picked up my first Fall
red leaves in years. Must have been
a frost. Is that how it is? I was last
in the U.S. before 9/11. Some Fall
there! Today, the clothes take longer
to dry outside. Despite being near
Madrid's latitude. Indeed, the sun's
still high at mid-day. And Civil
Wars are migrating, waiting on the
roadside wires. Keep in touch with
with sore sap as it wings down hard.

SUNLIGHT

Desirable, it was. And
now, forgotten sums
and formulae, it's in the darkest.

I can't leave. Sun screens it well
out. Or in. Hide it.
Think of the sun light as a hiding

place. Think of your body's skins
unfurled or flying
through the Northern lights uncatchable.

They were stretching the sky when Vietnam
was my worst fear. Draft
one in sub-atomic red.

CLOCK ON

Junk mosquito blood spreads wide on my hand.
Caught and processed in some factory farm
of my unwilling evolution. Would
anyone care? What's displayed in these clouds
of ethics all misty? Picture faces
in digital passports, finger printing
electronically, proof of real
identity in creepy vows before
the President. Love him, love them. All bound
to honour each small, defacing bite taste,
the sucked juice of revenge and capital
intuitive, standing upright in the
Draft Board local office, where card indices
rule. Carrying it always with nothing
but guilt, though its numerical place empowered
grand stats of hatred and warfare, clock on.

PUTTY

Some form of stupidity its
asking and telling beyond
silly playthings alarmed, stiff blood
ring, ring, so squeeze this, game on,
it's bodily fluids, had it
putty stops going on round,
I suppose it's quite satisfied,
already memorial
to heart, or hearts, now holding glass
windows in place with tacks and
linseed thumbed in the frame all round
as if in a house wall as

SPINNING TOP

Returning's like what it cannot, can't.
It's not there, wasn't ever,
I'm sure as can be. Before, wasn't there,
so relax the trashy sums.

Unspeakable bright insects presiding
is all I've got of conscience.
Long division's glowing hellmouth loves sun

in the South. Go for the bits
left over, left fruitless, left a spinning top
game-plan for ever and more.

I think the remainder will scorch
atoms when they're death or dead
again, flat similarities. Rise not
yet through backdoor universe.

'S A CONNECTION

Back at Elaine's childhood's house
for another summer like before, so
I put the chair down the end
of the mown patch to stare by the forest
through few still mysteries, just
the fraught dissimilarities joking.
All the un-allowed get stung
if you go in, got in, 's a connection.

PRINT OUT

I like the numbers folding in
to each other. Idea of them slipping in
or out as far as perfection.
Not that it would be, whatever is still wanted.
That's a live calculation run
out wild. Don't stop it. At your heart's finger tips you
go near a touched estimate of love to
breathe the end or near it; unfold, print out.

CLOSURE

Like free gravity
pushing as far as it can
and preparing to work tail-first. Slam
it's a musical
door latch, a spring closer,
so as not to let the sheep in with
their green chewed mess drops,
colours mathematical
and redundant for any future,
but fast tale-telling closure,
loving that fiction so long.

BIRDSONG ON MARS

Watch clouds for ever sussed out,
condensation for life or just this
second. Extend rough pressure
and air flow like organ bellows grind
through hot lips and tragedies.
The grey dripping curtains of rain dust
play fugues with talk certainty,
drop fall kisses on the hills beneath,
though that's a word of dross and rubbish.
It's fallen into birdsong on Mars.

ORDINARY

Contingency plans
unwieldy
to heave through any inner darkness or outer. Skin deep ways
to the Universe.
Weep! Come close.
Fix it if there's time. But just listen to that. If whatever,
in one second clamped
well down there,
in Mesopotamian sixties and circles, fly ordering.

INTENTIONS

Such edge of green flame invites
as does a hallelujah blast off for a tricksy
imaging ghost. Touch to hurt good
and hurt some more the nerve ends.
With no funeral that I went to it's still hunky
dory powerful and hot. Talking to
the silent surrounders' jet
pus sights they're listening and yearning to join up hands.
I love their desire. Such supersedes their
maths and logical grid lines
and undevout intentions.

SLOW MESSAGES. SLOW NERVES. STAFFA AGAIN. STOP

Do you live on another island? Good
enough for more spaces in your head. Fill
'em. Neuro chasms, the years of spacing

in the hard wires, I'm hungry. Messages
for bread, for breeding. Bakery orders.
I'm crying for my nerve fibres' doorways.

Boo hoo. It's all clotted cream and jam scones.
Getting there, got there. Home-made pharmacies.
Deliveries well-timed, like crusty loaves

to the battlements, sucked out messages
love their endings. Frightful enjambements

catapult to homeward paralysis.

Got there. Stop. Basalt. Stop. Columns. Stop. Stop.
Well-founded grammatical isolates.

DARKNESS

Islands in the drizzle over there not
visible this morning. Crass to watch
out. For them unvisitable.
Like gone again. Happy refuges while
away the time. Rough pencil and oil
paint anyone's retinal
seascape. Back in there, prisoner's wet cells,
their unhappy voyages a slow recall.
Rain loves a backyard brain.
Call them voyages? I doubt the sea legs'
fortunes. Rock with the swell out there in
the gaps. Partition off the
bell curves, water's proportion all slip-ups
in the calculus before it breaks
out into the open darkness.

WRITTEN SMELL

Cry, you fool, for my ankle.
Stop the trees, stop the steps, stop solemn
credulity. Love the stench.
Smells from under a bandage, war cries,
or war cries that claimed innards,
where the nearest bomb-shelter up the
road, and down slimy steps' old
pee-stink leaves, go comforting themselves,
since I wanted them to have
a purpose. The bomb dive's rot-drizzle
I gave a destiny: loam
to play with. And all so lightless and
dangerous. A sprain into
hell's mouth joins corruption's promise.

TROD. ROMANESQUE

This mock sonnet is substituting for simple slop and grandeur.
At first, it seemed an alternative to thinking of Sheffield, and
what then was steel and its words and architecture. Planted
in bombed territory. Nothing from whole memories except
journeys out and self-engendered pictures of victory in my head.
Or in a park. A part-bomb-proof park, pricked with weeds and
lupins and empty ponds. And a smell of old clothes and work.
All plaintive others, just so well trained in locality's names.

Blooms trod, slippy Romanesques' up-arched
stems' soles; I love their upside down pathways'
dripping cool tendrils to pace on, flush
with flat sky. Hang on to the Ionic
bits, the dazzling flower-pots' luscious
designs on anyone's glory. I'll crush
them easy, walking frayed coiling coats
of old sap. You're up there fleeing the roots
of heaven if it's up there, photo-
synthesis colouring up the blue vaults
to turn them green, a fine surgery's
colour; and far less frightening, and calm,
pending whatever operations
I've asked for to walk cleanly on my hands.

CONTRACT

Deep breath? Don't do it
if you wish to push or stand
through some dead metaphor's will.
My physio says
it's worthless, the feeling
strain isn't for oxygen's
service, no translation gas-free
through cell walls' tottering love.
Possessing the medics -
my doctor, my anaesthetist -
as though there'd be a contract
enforceable by law's
own muscular
presumptions.
Learn otherwise.
Learn deathly.

ANT TRAILS

Flawed medicine, so swallow it
mathematically per hour, per
day, so the sums add up and break
through, or down, the barriers. I think
of ant trails past deforming skin,
or reforming like prayers into
cell walls. Insects know the noisy
information beams all walkable.
Would that their patterns could be gelled
into digestible talking love
across the grass to be meaningful
with each gulp, to get it down whole.

GONE VIRAL

There's a blood-brain barrier's an odd
proposition. One squelch and it's gone.
All membranes' frailty. Working
on the bugs? Neah! Can't see it.
Epstein-Barr in feverish vessels
of blood disorders' viral mash up
just does for the walls and fences.
I imagine electric wires
to keep the cattle at home, playful
survival games with old DNA.
Moo, moo. Line up to digest the
charge. Would I make sense of numbers'
existential affair unbranded,
gone viral, as they say? Not me guv.

CAPTIVATING

Extraordinary fames, sad folios,
I'm there again, resenting *Samson*
Agonistes' GM crops. Ink, black ink, weighs
words at a perfect force to be sewn.
Don't fight it, I guess. They've bred fish oils
in plants to feed back to caged salmon.
What discoveries! All the language power
saved and sieved for holy fish farm food.
I'll be stunned, right between the eyes, set out in
thick paper. Such calculations can't
be fraudulent, the tragic drama's structured
out. Libraries' documents frying
as the sun heats up. Literature's brave.
Read it again in captivity print.

FUGAL

Wishfully fugal, specious. That way in
to the sheepfold. Bark! Guide them
in. Atomic dogs to think of,
untrained, but musical to silly
DNA. Get in there to
sound between the galaxies. Woof.
Settle in a nick of space-time quick.
Comfortable apprentice
tuners knock on, even in headless
stars. Learn, learn, learn, luck of vacant lots,
backdoor universals. I
want the logic, predatory
electrodes sparked, hunched, or hunkered on
old matter, wastage of band-aid sores.

UTTER

Rich parchment, and sealing rings, letting piss to the world's
utter transformation, chemically. Such
musculature to be added on, mostly; brainy
as the wastepipes leached through old galaxies' joints,
so a laugh a minute as if raining wild and glad
through paradise lost into e = m
c^2. Mockingly precise. Bilingual. No way out
except through some light catheter's tubular
messy transfers, past an eclipsing prostate's deep
lightless fry-up. What speed of vision cracks
with up-ended atoms! I love their intimacy,
not what they are, plain and simple, but how they
rule together making fire and heat and perpetual
anguish for disposal, the bells of orbital pain.

SCABS

The whole thing's volcanic so they say.
Old memories starve.
Would the lava have cared for
its legacy? Put a war down just
where its layout flops
through and over the strata's
edge. Hey! Molten edges reflect my
venom. Bite hard, bite
harder into survivors'
wrecked blood-flow. Walk tall, said my physio,
and don't think too hard.
It just needs you to happen so you
can see it. Pan round,
left to right, towards gigantic scabs.

SOLSTICE TINTED

The solstice at Calgary, the sea as
wide as it gets but it's cold and raining I
guess in time for Christmas. Celebrate old
photos tinted round the edges with pictures
and gin or gin and pictures. It's what we're
here for. I'll tell that again. It's a laugh to
pictorialize the ends of my limbs.
Put it back, the missing bits in arty framed
companionship. I'm looking for more rain
coming in from the east to blot shrieking bones
as they last for ever or until the
next sucker cries at being helped to stand
when it looks too bloody. Unfortunate
last tears guilty with the last fright enlargement.

Pipe work, blood work: such dramatic speech.
Off the map while shuffling down Broome to Spring to
the Cupping Room? Beat down the
roads. Primitive in the body so
akin to sewage. Goes around to below
ground. I've loved it with Soho
and Greenwich and Lower East and
West. Not sure now why it was so much worth the
knowledge of. On your ground floor
the Moonies' take-away's a land mark,
smells of fat, smells of faith gone stupid. Ahoy
there. The sea's not far. Road maps
are frightening everywhere. Get real.
Get where the bridges articulate.

THERAPEUTIC

Therapeutic forest, the forest to be
looked into or at or through, but why
'the'? Dense nonsense, as though specific trudge, nameable
with all its hooked bits. It'll get you sure with
all its dark, flawed, sweet berry traps and
mosquitoes. That'll teach you. Or 'larn' you. At school I
had, punishment for forgetting, to draw six
elephants complete with mahout and
howdah. They never forget their biology or
geography or where the widest deserts
were, or tundra or trees, or tree lines
going south or up high. I looked from the garden edge
to pine scrub invitations with spurious
comfort and coffee as though impugn.

FLORID

Did I think or want to
see looking
South each day further
into the insect patch
and mould stink?
Some patterns no doubt
in aesthetic formal
dredging spite
to get its own back
or my own back. Please. Pleased.
What love sense -
less. Genes, broken D
N A's florid mutations
into an afterlife pride.

NORTH WALL

The cold makes me feel better.
Though it's only as good as day
trips up the North Wall of the Eiger,
exhilarating but it
does no good. Just think of the drop,
in souvenir free fall hymn numbers
or well-known choruses of
moral immunity played from
beaches to glacier. Walkie-talk-
ies' fading signals – hearing
you. Though, if, but the messages
go slow. Do I like it this way, all
dependent on this second's
climate? No charge. Press button B.

GROVEL

Free delivery of repeat pre-
scriptions like a final line that
comes back or a church service.
No. I'm serious. Healing, holy,
halig in old English. Exams -
worthy rote learning to pass
and proceed. It's in the everyday
lingo that getting better's in
the chant. Grovel to the pharm -
any van driver: he makes all well.
Well, that's done, out of the Exam -
in ancient Rome to drugging
heart and love. It's got back to base so
perfectly, someone's dream of grammar.

The Shipping Bulletin is like radio's Big Ben though it isn't a
simile. They follow each other, broadcasting a small legacy of
empirical control. Embedded and safe, the full
forecasts at ten-to-one a.m. and five-twenty a.m. enact, if just
too staid below the satellites,
their sequence: 'Sea Areas', 'Coastal Stations' and 'Inshore
Waters'.

Geography, not long since continental drift
was mere speculation, though Empire's red
coloured the known. Old days. Blather by
heart and recitation of mine
working, steel rolling, fishing ports' boat numbers
and what they did and how. Not us, not yet,
not ever. Sextants' smelted and pressed
metallic sun heights and sun rise
way before the Apollos breached all known flights
and etched perspectives. Sleep well through it so
calculations can get on without
us knowing where the nets get pulled
or steel is hammered or fossilled ferns get picked
for fire iron conversion to airways disarmed.

I get there really, in comfort, each year, to the 'Hebrides', in
sight of 'Tiree Automatic', and, further on a whale-watching
trip, to 'Ardnamurchan Point'. It's a sort of fantasy by sea,
or 'on air', as the studio lights say. I believe. When we go, in
each nice summer, the Hebrides are a tour back-to-front.
There are weather reporting stations working automatically

to say how many miles of visibility
there are. (Remember those accidental messages across the
sea in *On the Beach*? From no one to the last living people).
I'm on Mull, yet again, and this year can't even shuffle to the
sea to dip my hand in. I can just see from Calgary machair to
the auto weather tower on Tiree at the airport.

Touch any permitted trance
or trope of stylish geography
as offered in quaint
imperfect denotation.
Feel I'm pleading for an erotic
landing place from air,
an airstrip there on Tiree,
it's visible from Calgary Bay -
Mull not Canada -
and every seven hours
or so on the Shipping Bulletin
from Coastal Stations
it speaks its automatic report
as though striking democracy fled.

Audible maps, shell sand and lichen cosmetic surgery, or rock
tattoos, to remind my digital camera of what was once under
control; landscapes of ex-dominion. Imported eucalyptus
thrive at Calgary ready for a photo print garden. I'm older,
I guess. Who wouldn't want the pleasant smell set down for
ever at home? World Service now on.

COGS

Small cogs wait, inevitable.
Wind, fool: brained crows splayed to sit,
nest-like, flurrying through
heirloom watch guts. Pecking order
a sorted experiment.
Try time in the sunlight.
No good for dark desires. Hammer
hot steel for coiled springs' blather
from coke heat for seconds
to measure out past a sundial's
truth. External? I wish. Weakened
I fear. Hooks and eyes zip
old hours' visibility,
mechanics of a lifetime.

WEIGHTED

A watch with slips of paper, stained
and written on, blithe names of dried out
owners, snapped in dull outer silver clothes,
remains a dedicated puzzle, laughing

since it can't be wound. I mean I'm laughing out
below my cased-in brain. Blood symmetries
out-live us. Or not. Who sees them now
or the day before? Silent ticks

and such, immemorial and
de-magnetised when Earth's poles swap ends.
Hide a name tag under continents that
tectonically budge each other with a

grand smile under the mountains' certainties,
brave weighted throughout a coffin's message.

There's a South wind today but it's cold.
Arctic circulation from the misplaced jet-stream's hoist.
It's up and down through the wrong
stratospheres. Without a pen, without a watch
writing's off. What, as such, a mis-placed
Gulf Stream? Procedural ink offers nowhere to go.
Unsure of tic toc summer
I'm fine tempted into listless cold, loveless
between isobars, or isotherms.
Wishing all curdled, it don't do no structures today.
Is it catastrophic? I'm
sure so. Writing's come back like old lava. Just
the right solution, in the water,
clarified, blood-brain barrier, cloud base.

My childhood bedroom wars filtered
through cot bars, old hot pee stink living
its honesty in the carpet.
Carpet, huh? Old rubbish, old toys prayed
for, prayed on, a Doctor, Doctor's
face in the doorway, a novelty
a difference from before the
day before's snow, an alternative
discovery's white, given cold,
white Doctor's hair still in the door way.
Detached, whatever colours, they were
cold, they were unspoken yellow toys,
OK a jaundiced, feverish
snowfield territory, swap touched.

BED BOUND

Into a ward straight away. Got it.
Privilege. Wait less. Time less. Memories fold
in, unfold, guardianship. Ticked boxes
for what's so wrong. Surgery you know it's owned
for this moving, illuminating,
enlightenment. Knife flashes past so quick, love
it, it's dark, it's bed bound, it's silent.
I'm still awake when the drugs come round, and corn
flakes and tea. No electricity
breaking wind, no systems for bodily pay
back, no clean exchange of energy
or atomic particles of energy in the
next timed shit. Metric weight sounds seriously
out of infancy and into the adult.

AMBULANCE

The invention of a good ambulance
must go back some, I thought, pushed bumping cold
to its back door. Delivery man -
cutlery drawer, or cold oven door.
It's open, metallic the hinges of life,
unlock it and see. Bottles of breathable
atomic rescue I might even want to
grasp. Comfort hardly. I didn't want to
know who last lay there, one hour before,
or who was to go next at the end
of the next shift of agony or broken
pipes or ducts or cellular breakages.
Try another design for a free death
experience lite. Cut it out briefly.

GUARD

It is a guard or Guard. Or Ward. I'm in it. Innit the history
of English? Alternatives or developments of 'W' or 'G' so
normal. The hospital breath to hide in. Wheeled in and
wheeled out, tucked in to hold blood just where it's supposed
to be. Drowsily through the necks and valves with high
or low pressure, squeeze on mate. Here I am to have it
measured. Keep the heat in, the pressure points unreddened,
the pulse counting on and on thank goodness. On the
records where it can be stacked for ever or until my next visit
to safety. Hold well such a journey of love. There I'm in it
still, or quiet as I can be. As quiet. Well as can be.

DRIVERS

Intrusion, I heard catheters
count in millilitres. Will I make
the target? Of all measurements, it's one
it's hard to do much about. Try harder to
drink. I'm queuing with my drivers
in A & E. Yes, they wait for each
of theirs to be admitted. But it hurts.
It's another doorway, all labelled and clean
though I shout inside my head if
I can be worthy of pain relief
or what might be an unnecessary
intrusion. I'm shouting in my head for dread's
worth of weight and capacity out-pained,
out-freed, out-feared, out-lasted so suck tears.

WALKING STICKS

For remembering Terezin,
a joint tribute to poems over time
by Elaine and Jon Glover

Looking At Drawings From Teretzin

We usually stand touching.

> Before stars of David, pinned to skeletons,
> Before the numbers sitting on boards, hung
>   above and around with coats,
> Then; no numbers, coats piled to be taken,

We stand, not touching.

The gallery is still with walkers watching their
>   shoes while they move as if toward a coffin.
Yet, at funerals, relatives pat backs and whisper,
>   'the mums, the coffin, the body so natural'.

And one, or some can replace one dead –
>   the functions at least.
But the numbers on the walls are not
>   a corpse in a polished coffin.

Sticks

It's a crutch. It's a stick. It's for walking
hopelessly, hand-held, squeezed tight
it's a pen; stir with it. Stir black language on the floor,

weighed. Weighed on like ink pressed down on paper
with so much thought or malice
or love from my heart pressed down through my arm-joints
earth-wards

as though ink was drained through a blind-hole-
catheter out, down someplace
to make a mark, stump, stump, stir, given as though I knew

where on earth this pressure was leading down.
Write the incomprehensible black words,
leaning on any surface crap – asphalt,

tar, papyrus, velum, milk -
and stir them into animal life, into human.

Pictures and Poems from Terezin
    Exhibited, Leeds, September 1965

Keep walking. Past the pictures
in their gallery. Why assign ownership? Don't know.
They're there. It's done. They're framed. As in coffins

labelled so you know whose past's
gone by. Well, you went by, or we did, walking records'
imaginary snaps handed on for

us unlucky viewers, our
trance in horror survived in mortifying visits.
Or for them or us? Problematized tears,

guts' viewing stamped on the floor.
Dated like birthdays or death days, supporting sticks,
crutches of grief to help process head-films

of funerals, their thirty-
five mil celluloid flicks past into past dead poems.

Sprocket Holes

Explain if you can, or want to know, how sprocket holes
managed the unseen passage
of blanks between the moving picture screens.

So slick, such silently cog-revolving projection,
so the shutter speed held out
the unhappy, the regretted, the bad.

Bloody definite articles as though you knew each
one, each item of solid
deficiency as missing in clockwork's

parts. So, say it's there if you have to. Grammar loves it.
Big pictures carry us through
as though we might know some truth from history.

Discount the originators. Who were they then to
object to being blanked out?

Lupins

Blessed is the lupin sown to thwart
what our soldiers' hands raised to the light:
a camp with no architectural style,
with a name like this, Treblinka,
and the unnameable, blessed be He, God.
(Jon Silkin 'Trying to hide Treblinka')

Unspeakable, gutless, quiet.
So, there was nothing to say or to be said for
any ears to hear. Walk into the art

as if the gallery were an
operating theatre. Where's the anaesthetist?
Put us out. Make it easy. Make it safe.

Count down till you're gone. I believe
it's the trick. It's matching dates, so it's ordered – sick
of learning satisfaction. Go to art

to make you vomit. If you don't
I guess you haven't seen it. Close your eyes today
and again. Jon Silkin wrote a poem

called 'Trying to hide Treblinka'. I guess that
he did what he could with lupins.

Re-Sus

De-guilt. De-rust. De-spoil. Swallow
hard if you can. Can't. A ward's protest
at culture brought in. Clean it off for a god's
sake can't you? Doubt it. Re-doubt. Remember it well

enough to cough on for a bit
longer. For a left-over art work
breeding infection – it's there inviting some
anti-biotic to stop Teretzin's re-sus

the re-susitation of hate.
I fear it's coming back. Forget it
quick to make it irrelevant? Synthesise
its actions or enzymes or fluid propellants

to number skin deep the mind's tattoos.
We looked in silence, we're old and still in there.

NOTE

In September 1965 we went to an exhibition of pictures and poems which had been collected after the Second World War from artists and poets who had lived in Terezin or Theresienstadt, north of Prague. The poems were by children. At first, Terezin had been a show-piece camp with a small section open for inspection by the Red Cross. It soon became a transit camp for those destined for Auschwitz.

The first poem, by Elaine Glover, appeared in Leeds' *Poetry and Audience* Vol. 13 No. 6, Friday 19 Nov 1965. There was a footnote to explain 'mums': a flower somewhat like a chrysanthemum, associated, in America, with funerals.

The later poems, by Jon Glover, were written in 2017. Alice Goodman kindly gave Geoffrey Hill's walking stick to Jon at the Memorial Event in Leeds.

It is probable that Geoffrey Hill also went to the Exhibition from Terezin in September 1965.

These poems in this format first appeared in *Stand* Vol. 15 No. 2 (214).

The giraffe said no. The giraffe regretted.
The snow kept falling and the animals elsewhere said
there wasn't much of interest. Oh me. Oh
my. We've a cardboard, five-foot children's giraffe back to
the window and mocking the snow. Could I think
of walking it? Here, its presumptions are worth a path
cleared. I've forgotten how shocking it is to
the body to have to spade what you want, though dared, iced
water, a décor of choice. I'm used to sit
waiting for it to go rather than transforming it,
in the world's oldest dialogues – digging is
free, or was. Blade or blades, I'll try to love you
in my head or imagination or anywhere
in this animal zoo, or plant house, dis-welcoming.

PAST

Where's my past? Grass blades. Crap. As just pointless
to even use the words. Works. Elephants quarrel.
Some delicacy. All the unrecalled
bods in the room. Or rooms. Absences turnabout

and view me again. Go on there. Ask it
again and again for some one located, land
visible and true. Trash. I want it back
to love the impossible. Back. Or did I write

have the impossible? Love/have. Pen strokes. Love/have.
Name the clothes OK? How will it be packed?
Huh? Animals like snowstorms make for the ugly
body sitting here. Storms sitting? No such

trash again. I love it all gone and at my neck
like a cough in the outside surrounding
Remains of Elmet, Tarka the Otter, traps of
today's new snowfall and wiping them out.

I watched my brother dissect a frog.
Rat next week. Formaldehyde
freshened the night-time kitchen. Spread skin out-reeked
tea-time's chips. Old fats matured before our very eyes

as if competing for attention. Touched: muscles' bled
cognition of vacant stomachs' needs, a joke
IQ for all I knew of
surgery or cookery, freedom

to be curious, to be wild and
sort of experimental.
He pinned out arteries, I wrote up the books
or read Keats's letters on Guys' theatre's decayed air,

or have I made up paper's textual stench?
Wilfully configuring stitches' hold?

GOING OUT. RIGHT OUT

As it were ice. Needles
are asking for it. Flesh dead for now. Breathlessly
as though, as if cuddlesome blood

flows as if the tide were,
had had enough. Suck it and see, though the descent
couldn't be bothered to touch down.

Like a plane and pilot
all agreeing on landing right there, holy smoke,
holy cow, holy mackerel,

the operation flayed,
or flared like a torch illuminating heartbeat,
the pressures going up and down,

uncommanded if crystalline, infinitely
stripped, the anaesthetist's conversational tone.

INTO THE ARCHIVES
mock sonnets for Stella Halkyard

After viewing, handling, being mystified by
Dom Sylvester Houédard's archivist's
dream world, the paper shapes that no
real student of Eng Lit allowed his or her
head to believe in, OMG tattered
causalities in a Library
not. But an archive maybe for the deed transfers
in and out of existence; grave-digging
or hiding, the unexamined
relics we've all got to go to if we aren't burned
up. In another room Stella found a
black box, as, I'd no idea what
it was, an extra treat of academe
in acid free tissue *Our Photographs*,

my first Carcanet book MS
preserved like a good essay mark to share around.
It's what archivists do: they make all real.
Tho' I fear the philosopher's
fascination with the inaudible crash in
some forests or some delicate written
love solution scratched into brave
dead timber one hundred yards distant microfiled
and still illegible whoever might
follow today's students. How long?
That long, for ever. Black box two thousand, threaded
like time through cement in a bricked up
wall of dead tree knowledge layered in.
Don't plead optimism. Stella's found it unclicked.

The twenty-six poems that follow were written in about three weeks, 23 April – 18 May 2020. Sometimes, two or three were started in a single day. My wife Elaine Glover died in September 2019 after a few months illness which was only diagnosed in her last weeks as caused by Secondary Cancers. These were untreatable and inoperable. The Primary Cancer may have been a long term 'Silent' Ovarian tumour. Elaine came from rural Upstate New York near the shore of Lake Ontario and Niagara Falls. She went to Elmira College, NY, where one of her tutors, John Carthew, encouraged her to write poetry and to take her Junior Year Abroad at the University of Leeds where we met. Writing and working with the magazine *Stand* kept us together from 1965, when Jon Silkin entrusted us with running the magazine, while he went to the Edinburgh Festival, till her death. The poems are what I call 'mock sonnets'. They usually have to deal with the most intimate details of the dying process and stick within fourteen or sixteen lines. I chose a random pattern of repeating syllables per line so long as the whole thing ended up near 140 or 160. The patterns were different for each poem but patterns there were. The advantages (could there be any advantages in the circumstances?) may have been that the limitations encouraged a swift, detailed look at some problem – be it neurological or emotional – and then permitted, or revealed, how to move on. Or stop. Usually – halt. Elaine gave me everything, and her loss has been awful. I hope that these mock sonnets may allow some conversation between us to continue.

The sequence of poems is continuing, and I hope that more will be published, in journals and the next book(?), which explore Elaine's relationship with our daughters, Abigail and Rhiannon, our grandchildren, Alice, Oliver, Jake, Katie and

Lizzie, and her family in New York, especially her sister Nancy.

An obituary appeared in the *Guardian* (6 December 2019) and there were tributes in *Stand* Vol. 17, No. 4 2019 224. This issue also contained rediscovered poems from the 1960s by Elaine.

Pandemic

My kitchen door's
not safe, with parcels' chucked by, heaped
packaging I imagine might have squeezed new flu
bugs, half known in panic fiction, and read before midnight's traps shut
scared, oiled, drained down
maths and data's graphed predictions.
Do I, can I, love you more for dying way out
back in last September? Out back in the garden and the bins, soothed
gentle grass cuttings smooth to rot in the sun, so easy to fright,
to mock; don't touch
your face or eyes;
consumption for someone bodily preserved, or waiting time-wise
to be helped, to be cared for, don't
touch, de-mask, de-apron, de-glove.

My Mum's 1920s Hospital, Research

After the Great War, or during its ending, flu
spread so deathly quick. Trenches, advances, priceless
wards aligned all over till they
and it died out again. Research
in the Path Lab, Mum, with samples of nerves
and cold tissue in sections on slides waiting light.
Study, annotate the nerves' now
clear, bright stasis. Can we bother
who they belonged to? Nerves' rites of ownership brilliantly tagged for
the record. Is someone doing it all again in the Path Lab
down the road? Don't
breathe it in or
out. Her polished, quite sacred, microscope
unboxed from mahogany. Lies or true?

Cancer or Virus

BBC websites offer
click links I think or maybe some
Guardian copy to local deaths near
you. How many, how few - would that I didn't
want or need to know. Screen-time and virus life
I'm truly worried that some system's checking life's
worthiness and affections. DNA's stickiness
see it give up, give in when breathing stops, oxygen's glue
patched to your identity.
I love you for ever and more
in this primitive or futurist
now time of virus fields. Battles losing.
Metaphors ain't happy, kick their trellis work,
stain their pages. They don't know love so leave them be.
Names so needful and they're unstoppable, hospitals
go viral in wordsearches. On I love.

Flying

Inside the front window I'm stuck. Love two bird tables
to envy or admire. Claws
don't care. Nuts and artificials, corn seeds and sunflower
hearts – which neighbours tell me are
special for bullfinches. Some trysts or seductions net
old colours. No hummingbirds
here. Front window doesn't open on America.
Simple loves, no nibbles held
in cages. No imagined tastes worth pecking for. I'm
dulled to death. Flat Atlantic
come to me please. I'll walk it gratefully please
through Marie Curie's booklet on the
processes of dying, observable times,
events nearing breathlessness, flying.

Maths

To be loved always,
by stretching the garden into the forest walkways,
puts you there for good.
Priceless, snowdrifts or sunshine, it goes on in brain cells'
mathematics. Sum it up, and pathways resolve
anything they choose. Do you believe destiny?
my carer asked this
morning travelling
through books and papers free
to add or subtract times
tables and flesh. I didn't, I don't, I only choose
to sit there and look. Best poems come home, so ink them
in and type them up. No bending petals' digits to eat and drink
what I love of you answering the calculatings hopefully.

Electric Sleep

The technicals brought a hospital
electronically inflating mattress
for you to change the pressure on your
body's pressure points. So to be no pressure
there then. Minutes and more to be loved
so the screen says. And as you got out and in
again you had to be held up while
the technics entered your needs. A human blood
pressure cuddle round your arms so
you couldn't walk or fall or be removed from here.
We were hardly used to these lights
and their digitised pace through the frameworked new night
when you left it behind and chose a less
predictable way to freedom, countless.

   for Michael Schmidt

Beloved

Other forests waiting, I love
the deciduous, the evergreen, the palms and
nuts dropping or not, falling or
not. Awaiting. For some rooted patterning trust
bright dirt when you dig it up, soil
here, dirt there, fork it, divide 'n' choose bereavement
so surprisingly offering
an end that no one wants today; bough, sap down-flow
sagging the sightless, aimless trends
of deforestation. I feel I'm in there close
up and still. Ordnance Survey green space
no buildings or outlined roads or bench marks' heights
to co-ordinate or triangulate dead
on, though well spyed, well marked, well beloved.

Diary Entries

Appointments aren't always available. Time slots, death slots, rehab slots, drugs and relief slots. 'Bring you coffee?' When for you, for me, for the kids to watch and give? Perhaps not a question but a statement. It will be then, probably. What a plan to go into for coffee.

Journalism – dash
I didn't keep a diary of loss,
why ask now? Those lost events screech out sometimes
and, placeless, time-free, here now for good no worthy metaphor
answers back. I'd steal
from you like the solved answer to *pi*
like our last words, impossible similes,
have fallen between and between, no similarities spark
or tell or plead or
cry. I cry – dash, personal pronoun
I see in Grammar Books stands for something else.
'Stands for' – dash, I love and Secondary Cancer, the Prime was
Silent. As though, a substitute again,
– dash, thus unspeakable, unrecalled. Diary.

A nurse called at 8.20 in the morning to say her breathing had changed and I should get there. By 9.00, I think, when I got to the Hospice she had gone. The usual daily advice was to keep speaking to her. It seemed still right and still does.

Not, childish, able to do the sums, killed
lots then of what's now love. Killed before? Now
to register absence, so I should have known you'd go some time.
Hard still to think that nurse would know so much pre
blank space; time to phone, to know what's to

be done. Charges in
or out. To pay in electricity, metered in or out
the costs my love and yours. When I got there you
were still warm. Charged. I like to think
from starlight. Your share
my share. Too easy to cash in black holes, or metaphorise
the missing. So no go there. I've had it all
down the Hospice's bent corridors,
a door glass shuttered.

Remains

Disremembered. That *Diary Week*
to view A5. Smith's choosing how it's to be seen.
Passing, till you get a new one
now or January, just waiting to fill in
clear lines with what happened then and
for ever. It's love of infinities, trouble,
breathless to the end. But where will
that be? This bed's timed results, where will they be now
near the bathroom, the ends of ideas to play with
showering so necessary
water's a blank space waiting to be added to
why can't I help? Your histories,
in the drains. Washing with your carer's hands
gently what's weighty, the faecal remains.

Years Ago Appleton NY

Mornings in Appleton I chose not
to switch on the radio. No newspapers
I went each day to the end of the garden
to write at the edge of the forest. No fence, hedge
or wire. Property speechless, birds,
rimless, paperless. Knowledge spitting
what the trees chose. If they did that day look
at my finger-nails and ball point and coffee
cup. For now no war knowledge cackle
a quick maths hairspring zig zag zig serene
family get-together They spoke I was sure
though I was quite alone, like now. Together in
the kitchen with coffee. No moves
permissible but Appleton's here, surely so.

◆

Mock

Artifice, like heartbeats, so long, so many work
behind and underneath. Spoof wood work
just like Mock Tudor in your veins
to process to the ground, vain
and rotting weather vane
I think my electronic watch doesn't like work.
It would like to rot it is so vain
it would close its battery not work
in front of my eyes, wrist veins
pulse its broker fat vane
as a direction not to follow, dancing mock turtle
mock orange perfume assembles for dying improvement.

Times Tables

No distraction.
Not allowed. No music or voice
to mean anything other than you know. Knowing
what's here is justly distrustful. I'm counting railway stations pass
in my head not
really so no need to exit
to guilt, to fright, to the unlimited minus
signs in your brain neurons' junction boxes going to sleep with toys
with rules that are cuddly, with barred unknowns of loveliness to yearn
for. Think of breathing not needed nor eating nor
sight, nor liquid; the chemistry's
gone slow, it's got
all. It's doing its silent maths, deduction after deduction
it's getting it right as thought it's really happy
de-energising to the end
times tables flat

Log Tables

A&E: guess now few from the virus
world. Where my brother worked and my nephew
works now. Sort the queues, help them cope
with frights. I filled forms for Elaine
though she reported in before this new world's sums.
I wonder where the form's stacked now? To be found for
stats, for history, for love's kindly touch -
it was there for anyone, quick to see.
No dozing in triage or post
scan notes. Are you in print still here?
The bad news or no news in data. Get out now
and wait in the car park. Its hoarding charges lift
the spirit. Patient, patiently
wait a vacancy, turn the log tables smartly.

So Long

Inaudible nerve endings cut,
how curt neurons' delicious pitch,
so the ends love each other, touch your hand,
touch your knuckles, the dead weight conduction
for your electrical messages, their wish lists'
for home-ward, home-based plugs and sockets your eyelids
need a call to sort the mis-fit
the voltage dis-loves, dis-proves, dis-
allows. Circuit breakers unhealable -
imagine a hospital, the whole thing,
to re-join one nerve. It's all in my pictorial
communication with your eyes, and eyelids, ears
and old voltage discharges shock
waves' screen to love so long as, screen to love so long

Physics

You lay in total silence. 'In' what compartment would you have lain?
What's unconscious like? No wakening, no pain, no sound? No
spoken love gets in, though the doctors all said keep
talking. Locked in too much and close even
for the secret vibes to say hello.
Imagine a thunder
clap along an axon, a whisper in a frontal lobe precise
and quiet enough to make the storm just friendly to the lips.
From inside, what's your world? Stop think world and treasure
stuff. Stop it. You've given me – past tense, no string
or ribbon or photos or cards.
Past tense in lingo, sex
given, gave, touched there in your head.
Sees silent cage of bird feed suet, worms
contains food stuff, and their tiny feet still hang on
long enough to peck and nip where light physics' speech has got.

Signs

Signs. Such as wanting water are surely
readable. We know the traffic lights when to start
or stop. I love your thirst out loud;
it's a dictionary of nerve endings
and eyesight, our history back on the bookshelf
if I'm not careful. She'll not want
thirst any more. Don't think of force feeding.
Is it like prison? Well, no outside world, nor in
known either. So sort of. But no
gates or doors or ceremonial admission.
No signs to read or obey or record. Quiet,
so systematic, so content,
so much there for others to love
and distinguish from logic or signage.

Delaying

Delaying
though I didn't know. So it's useful body fat, self-satisfying
energy gets on by, formulaic
transcendence. So still graced after a night;
I greet you
standing next to your silence and your slower breathing moving next
to your well tucked bed. A safe night now gone
and doctors kept checking to make it well,
cellular growth in
darkness, dividing a few more times, though leaving more nerve ends
well behind, just lost
counts uncaring for more electric pulses, images used
or used up. Were there built in pictures known
in whatever last dream, you ask, I ask.

Tight Lipped Primary

It might have been silent ovarian cancer that started it.
They said, near the
end. Though it wasn't 'they' it was 'he' or the nice quiet 'she' Doc.
Metaphors we
prefer. Though do we? A vote on silence near the start of new life
I suspect would
stay uncounted or shouted out in tears or mystified unvoiced,
its children so
quietly confident went walkabout. And did start some mumbling
to ask questions
so disquieting, so repetitive.
Your Notes Say How Are You Today
And When Did This Start And How To Answer
In Silence, From Silence Tight Lipped.

Scans

A CT
Scan doesn't show brain inflammation, so deluded, so troubled they
tried again
with MRI but you couldn't consent to entering that hole in
the machine, and you screamed. So the Primary
stayed unproved. Who wanted to know what
should be in the Notes as causation? Did you?
So could any love bye-pass the blots,
the nerves that not long ago gave extreme pleasure
to you and me in their own ways,
a disconnect with all the maths coming out wrong,
to sleep then happened without a
dispute? No brain scanning needed for love,
sex or death, imagery, metaphors, not.

Cold Blanket

Next under the cold blanket seen
as dressed up for a higher examination,
though no questions worth long answers.
Electricity preserves your pulled back certain
smile. Loved, I wonder, for now, how
to speak to your body from out the Hospice fridge,
though I need to stand right next to
you, for fear, for love, for ownership, though to give
you away just needs me to leave
your humming bedside and this room.
Signatures to collect. Their job, their duty done
I want to go back in time. Though who do I ask?
Words live repeatedly – come back – to-from
unheard, unseen, refrigerator's space.

Calgary or Appleton

Calgary
the first sand to play in or on when you were babies became magic
memories
and we went back often though in sunshine camping you both got sunburned
and in the evenings got midge bitten
till we lifted the tent pegs to retreat
down South lost
till the year after next which was Appleton and poison ivy threats
don't explore
the forest out back or you might end up in hospital like your Mum
did as a kid. Elaine's only hospital
stay till now. And your births. Such different
pains before
its silent vacations in a newly discovered continent's drift.

for Abigail and Rhiannon

Infirmary

A place to greet or to say goodbye Infirmaries love their places
mapped, head placed,
got memorised for ever as the location of the kind people
and your births
on documents, proofs of identity,
how you learned to hold on to thirst as love
and holding on for ever so it seemed, till counting out sleep time, suck
time alone
didn't work and you had to help me to say goodbye and to love but
what was left.
Thank you, I held you first, in the labour
ward and the ambulance, mapping out the
truth that you're here with all Elaine gave you, counting in your lips, fingers
and eyesight

For Abby in the Labour Ward and Annie in the Ambulance. And now.

Gave Birth

They helped to get the wheelchair to
the ambulance. Stairs, edges, doors don't
agree. For the drivers it's normal to
go. To slow stairlift and from stairlift tight skin
talks. Elaine, it was me who couldn't do actions.
Clothes frighten. Steps frighten. Just words.
You couldn't plead for your legs to be
moved, for the journey and out again down.
Did I, who was just as stuck too, help you or
the driver in or out of disbelief? No way,
through more doors to officially
be counted just as helpless, more forms
more vocab the drivers used day and night
to a bay for unconsciousness, reporting
through straps and adhesive gauges to help them to
care and know. Annie joined us and Abby,
just a few feet from where she gave you birth.

Fittings

Jeff and Nancy, thanks for coming, none of us knew
it was to say goodbye though, of
course, you said goodbye when you left each day
and Nancy back to New York. Bye.
Poetry, pictures, old symmetries, like you live in Jefferson
or Didsbury,
places for the times and the time going, would it be a comfort
to love the gone?
Subtracted from time-space from consciousness out
spoken, out-told, and out-listened out
done by History and its names. Out-silenced, stop it
now. Does our love in the doorway
always cross out the sums? You were here, here
to add, here to add planks, locks and fittings.

Audubon

Tense is awful
for any conversation now. I want no past, no transaction
mirrored that way.
Give it here, give it back, see it? The edge of the hospital bed
was raised for safety though when you
wanted me to get in for a familiar
feeling I could just but I could
not stay for what you wanted. Perfect or future
perfect tenses
recalled for us to enact, get it right, to be like the still birds
in Audubon's
so loved details that you wanted badly to see in your body
still painting yourself into still anatomy
unlearning touch to do without

Back to the Beginning

To sit with us from marriages
so different but part of our lives they flew in
or drove round. Judith and Jackson
from thousands or twenty miles, visibility's
what counts. Adding up seen times held
as if or like or instead of ceremony.
No one asks if you've to be dead.
But presence across the time boundaries lives clear
and simple. Get on a plane or
Motorway to rehearse the state of our marriage
tickets please, fuel re-filled, safety checks done
it lets us all lift off for a moment
till we all go on back go on
how back to the beginning, if not, how just now?